the Lost Teachings *of* JESUS *on*

---

the SACRED PLACE *of* WOMEN

Other Books by Alonzo L. Gaskill

Love at Home:
Insights from the Lives of Latter-day Prophets

The Truth about Eden:
Understanding the Fall and our Temple Experience

Sacred Symbols:
Finding Meaning in Rites, Rituals & Ordinances

The Lost Language of Symbolism—An Essential Guide for
Recognizing and Interpreting Symbols of the Gospel

Odds Are You're Going to Be Exalted—Evidence that the
Plan of Salvation Works!

Know Your Religions, Volume 1—A Comparative Look at
Mormonism and Catholicism

the Lost Teachings *of*
JESUS *on*

the SACRED PLACE *of*
WOMEN

ALONZO L. GASKILL

CFI
An Imprint of Cedar Fort, Inc.
Springville, Utah

ISBN 13: 978-1-4621-1390-3

Published by CFI, an imprint of Cedar Fort, Inc., 2373 W. 700 S., Springville, UT 84663
Distributed by Cedar Fort, Inc., www.cedarfort.com

LIBRARY OF CONGRESS CATALOGING-IN-PUBLICATION DATA

Gaskill, Alonzo L., author.
The lost teachings of Jesus Christ on the sacred place of women / Alonzo L. Gaskill.
    pages cm
Includes bibliographical references and index.
Summary: Explores doctrine about women and their divine role that was lost from the Bible and restored in these latter days.
ISBN 978-1-4621-1390-3 (alk. paper)
1. Women--Religious aspects--Church of Jesus Christ of Latter-day Saints. 2. Notovitch, Nicolas, 1858- Vie inconnue. I. Title.
BX8643.W66G37 2014
289.3'32082--dc23
                2013044930

Cover design by Shawnda T. Craig
Cover design © 2014 Lyle Mortimer
Edited and typeset by Emily S. Chambers

Printed in the United States of America

10 9 8 7 6 5 4 3 2 1

Printed on acid-free paper

For my daughters, Rachael and Kathryn,
that you may see yourselves as Christ sees you—and in the hope that the men in your life will always treat you as the Savior would.

And for my sons, Gary, Keaten, and Jared,
that you may see your mother, your sisters, your wives, and your daughters as God sees them—and in the hope that you will always treat women with the reverence and respect a man of God would.

CONTENTS

Acknowledgments

I wish to gratefully acknowledge the assistance of my able research assistant, Michael Duval, whose help on this project has been invaluable. His hours of research, given in the spirit of consecration, have blessed my life and have advanced this project. When I think of Michael, I am reminded of the words of President Brigham Young: "To me it is the Kingdom of God or nothing. . . . Without it I would not give a farthing for the wealth, glory, prestige and power of all the world combined" (*Journal of Discourses* 11:126). Thank you, Michael, for your service, friendship, and example!

As always, I express my sincere appreciation to Jan Nyholm for her editorial assistance. Over the years, she has improved the quality of my work via her able red pen. It is rare to find a soul so willing to serve. When President Kimball stated, "God does notice us, and he watches over us. But it is usually though another person that he meets our needs" (*Ensign*, Dec. 1974, 5), surely he had Jan Nyholm in mind.

Finally, my heartfelt gratitude goes out to my friend Aaronita Card. Her pre-publication review of the text and her helpful suggestions have greatly improved the manuscript. I am reminded of the words of Sister Elaine Jack, General Relief Society President of the Church, who said, "No greater heroine lives in today's world than the woman who is quietly doing her part" (*Ensign*, Nov. 1990, 89). Sister Card, thanks for your heroic life and example!

INTRODUCTION

Of all people, Latter-day Saints should be the most reverential of women and their sacred place within the Church, the family, and God's "great plan of happiness" (Alma 42:8). Our understanding is unlike that of the rest of the world, and thus our women should be different from the world, as should be the way our men treat the fairer sex.

Sisters lead within the Church, presiding over the Relief Society, Primary, and Young Women's organizations. The work that takes place in the classes and activities of those organizations is often *quite literally* life changing. The building and nurturing of testimonies is a sacred responsibility admirably carried out by faithful, consecrated Latter-day Saint sisters.

Within the walls of the holy temple, sisters who have entered into sacred covenants perform saving ordinances on behalf of God's children by God's authorization. In so doing, they act as symbols of Christ—blessing, attending to, and serving their sisters on both sides of the veil.

In the family, alongside their husbands, mothers guide, teach, and nurture their children, helping them to develop their talents and testimonies, their characters and their conduct. We must not underestimate the influence of a righteous mother's teachings, love, and example upon generations of her posterity.

Central to the divinely revealed plan of salvation is this profound truth, so beautifully articulated by Eliza R. Snow:

In the heav'ns are parents single?
No, the thought makes reason stare!
Truth is reason; truth eternal
Tells me I've a mother there.

When I leave this frail existence,
When I lay this mortal by,
Father, Mother, may I meet you
In your royal courts on high?[1]

Latter-day Saints believe in the divine parentage of every human being. We acknowledge God, our literal and eternal Father in Heaven. And, with reverence, we also acknowledge our literal and eternal Mother in Heaven. Just as faithful men manifest the attributes of the Father, so also women who seek to live up to their divine birthright manifest the characteristics of our loving, eternal Mother. It is the destiny of each man and woman to become as God is. As C. S. Lewis so famously stated, "It is a serious thing to live in a society of possible gods and goddesses, to remember that the dullest and most uninteresting person you talk to may one day be a creature which, if you saw it . . . you would be strongly tempted to worship"[2] because he or she had lived up to his or her divine potential. This is our call—our destiny!

This little book is both a testament to the sacred place of women and an invitation to men and women of the Church. To the sisters, it is a summons to live out your divine role—to be what God has called you to be: good, holy, loving, exemplary, and godlike. To the brethren, it is a call to treat God's daughters as He would treat them: with admiration, respect, gratitude, love, and awe. As President David O. McKay noted, "There is nothing so sacred as true womanhood."[3] This little work is a testament to the reality of that prophetic declaration.

Of course, within the pages of this short book we speak of the ideal that each faithful follower of Christ might wish to achieve. And, as members of The Church of Jesus Christ of Latter-day Saints, we earnestly seek the ideal. But we also acknowledge that each of us is a work in progress. No Latter-day Saint should feel badly that he or she falls short of perfection so long as that brother or sister is continuing to progress and seek each day to become just a bit more like God and Christ. Exaltation is not an event; it is a process! The truths taught within the pages of this book are representative of what God would have each of us—male and female—strive for. But in so doing, He would remind us that the very purpose of the Atonement of Christ is to make up for our shortcomings—to make up for the areas wherein we *do* fall short of the ideal. Thus, the reader is invited to look for principles herein with which he or she resonates and, *with the help of Christ,* to strive for application of those principles. This is decidedly *not* a book about what you're doing wrong. It is a testament to what we, through God's help, can do right and to what we, with His help, can become.

The LOST TEACHINGS of JESUS—the ORIGIN of the TEXT

In the year 1887, only a decade after the Turko-Russian war, journalist Nicholas Notovitch (himself a Russian) took an extended trip to the subcontinent of India. In a detailed memoir of his journey, Notovitch recorded, "In the course of one of my visits to a Buddhist [monastery], I learned from the chief Lama that there existed . . . in the archives of Lassa . . . very ancient memoirs, [which spoke] of the life of Christ."[4]

This monastery, a Tibetan Buddhist cloister, is located in northern India, in Hemis, Ladakh (within the Indian state of Jammu and Kashmir). According to Notovitch, the monks had a number of documents dating back to the first century, manuscripts that not only contained information on the life of Christ, but which also chronicled some of His most sacred teachings.

Upon learning of the documents, Notovitch became intrigued and pressed his hosts to allow him to view the ancient texts. However, he indicated that as he asked questions about the scrolls, his "persistent inquiries . . . aroused suspicion in the minds of the lamas." Each time the subject arose, they were "on their guard" and spoke with hesitancy in response to Notovitch's "efforts to gain information."[5] The journalist began to doubt the reality of the scrolls, or at least his ability to ever access their content.

Notovitch soon left the monastery with the intention of returning some time later to inquire again about the documents. However, in a rather fortuitous accident, shortly after his departure he was thrown from his horse, fracturing his femur just above the knee. This injury prevented him from traveling for some time. Thus, of necessity, he was carried back to the monastery, where he remained under the care of the monks until he was able to continue his journey. During his extended stay, he apparently ingratiated himself to the chief lama, who eventually consented to read the texts to Notovitch as he lay incapacitated. As the words that the Lama read were translated by Notovitch's guide and interpreter, the journalist recorded the content of the documents verse by verse.[6] The words of Christ recorded in these manuscripts stunned the Russian visitor.

According to the monks, the content of these ancient texts was acquired by some Indian merchants who had been in Judea during the last year of Jesus's mortal ministry. Shortly after Christ's crucifixion, these itinerant importers returned to their homeland and told of the truths they had seen and heard. Within three or four years of Christ's death, the testimonies of these eyewitnesses regarding Christ were recorded. Consequently, if their report is true, then their record of Jesus's teachings was penned *before* any of the four Gospels.[7] Over time, the records of Christ's teachings were brought from India to Nepal and then eventually taken from Nepal to Tibet, where Notovitch first learned of them.[8]

Though the texts had been among the monastics of Tibet for centuries by the time Notovitch arrived, the vast majority of lay Buddhists were ignorant of their existence and content. Jesus (or "Issa," as the Buddhist lamas call Him[9]) "is not recognized as one of the principal saints in Tibet." The chief lamas were the only ones who apparently retained knowledge of Him because they were the only ones who had access to the scrolls that told of His life, teachings, and torturous death.[10]

As Notovitch poured over these lost teachings of Christ, he recognized that much of their content was not found in the writings of the New Testament evangelists, and yet they were "remarkable for their character of divine grandeur."[11] They professed to be "sublime words" from the Master Himself, and the Spirit seemed to accord.[12]

Our focus within the pages of this book will be on a singular discourse attributed to Christ and purported to be discovered by Notovitch on that fateful day in 1887.

Latter-day Saints have a long history of being fascinated with inspired texts that have somehow not made their way into the standard works of the Church. For example, the Prophet Joseph Smith was drawn to the Book of Abraham—though many of its stories were not found anywhere in the Bible or Book of Mormon. He sensed the Spirit of that text when he first encountered it, and he wanted the Saints to also see and feel the power and value of that book—even though, in Joseph's day, it was not considered scripture.[13] Likewise, the Lord informed the prophet of the value that could come to members of the Church from studying the Apocrypha *by the Spirit*—though it also is not part of our scriptural canon

(See D&C 91:1, 5). The prophets and apostles—ancient and modern—have been quite clear that there are *many* inspired works that have not made their way into our scriptures, but from which we can gain strength and inspiration as we read them by the Spirit.[14] Jesus's lost teachings on the sacred place of women seems a prime example of one such text. Its encouragement to men is to reverence women and treat them as God would. Its counsel to women is to live worthy of such reverential treatment. Though the location of the written discourse at the time the Bible was compiled prevented its inclusion in our New Testament, the Spirit of the Lord attests to the truthfulness of the teachings contained therein.

The LOST TEACHINGS of JESUS—the DISCOURSE

V:9 Whosoever respecteth not his mother, the most sacred being after his God, is unworthy of the name of son.

V:10 Verily I say unto you: Respect woman, for she is the mother of the universe, and all the truth of divine creation dwells within her.

V:11 On her depends the whole existence of man, for she is his natural and moral support.

V:12 She gives birth to you in the midst of suffering. By the sweat of her brow she rears you, and until her death you cause her the gravest anxieties. Bless her and adore her, for she is your only true friend and support on earth.

V:13 Respect her, protect her. In acting thus you will win her love and her heart. You will find favor in the sight of God and many sins shall be forgiven you.

V:14 In the same way, love your wives and respect them; for they will be mothers tomorrow, and each later on the ancestress of a race.

V:15 Be submissive toward your wife. Her love ennobles

man, softens his hardened heart, tames the brute in him, and makes of him a lamb.

V:16 The wife and the mother are the inappreciable treasures given unto you by God. They are the fairest ornaments of existence, and of them shall be born all the inhabitants of the world.

V:17 Even as the God of hosts separated of old the light from the darkness and the land from the waters, woman possesses the divine talent of separating in a man good intentions from evil thoughts.

V:18 Wherefore I say unto you, after God your best thoughts should belong to women and to wives, woman being for you the temple wherein you will most easily obtain perfect happiness.

V:19 Here you will forget your sorrows and your failures, and you will recover the lost energy necessary to enable you to help your neighbor.

V:20 Do not expose her to humiliation. In acting thus you would humiliate yourselves and lose the sentiment of love, without which nothing exists here upon earth.

V:21 Protect your wife, in order that she may protect you and all your family. All that you do for your wife, your mother, for a widow or another woman in distress, you will have done unto your God.[15]

COMMENTARY on the DISCOURSE

VERSES NINE, TEN
& THIRTEEN

Whosoever respecteth not his mother,
the most sacred being after his God,
is unworthy of the name of son.
Verily I say unto you: Respect woman,
for she is the mother of the universe, and
all the truth of divine creation dwells within her.
Respect her, protect her.
In acting thus you will win her love and her heart.
You will find favor in the sight of God
and many sins shall be forgiven you.

The Summary of the Sermon

While each of us is literally the spirit offspring of our Father in Heaven, the doctrine of Christ teaches that we must seek adoption into the family of Christ, spiritually becoming His sons and His daughters through faithfulness to covenants and through faith in His power to save. King Benjamin taught his people, "And now, because of the covenant which ye have made ye shall be called the children of Christ, his sons, and his daughters; for behold, this day he hath spiritually begotten you; for ye say that your hearts are changed through faith on his name; therefore, ye are born of him and have become his sons and his daughters" (Mosiah 5:7).

In Christ's lost teachings on the sacred place of women, we are informed that mothers are sacred in the divine plan. They are created in the image of God (Genesis 1:27). Whether man or woman, boy or girl, if we wish to be adopted back into the family of God—if we wish to become Christ's sons and daughters—we must be spiritually reborn. And a sure mark of spiritual rebirth can be found in how we regard those who have given us life: our God, who gave us spiritual life, and our mothers, who have given us mortal life.

Here Christ commands us to regard our maternal ancestor in the way that He does—as second only to our God. So much did Christ love and respect His mother that even in the hour of His suffering—as He hung upon the cross amid torturous pain—He tended to the needs of His mother (John 19:26–27). One worthy of the title son (or daughter) must hold sacred the beings who have made him such—his mother and his God. There can be no salvation for a child who does not love and respect his mother.[16]

Jesus offers us a profound promise for seeing the women in our lives as He sees them. He assures us that as we respect our mothers, wives, and women generally, we will not simply win their love, but we will win God's love and the remission of our sins! Could we wish for any greater gift?

Counsel to Men & Children

The words of this verse were echoed by the First Presidency of the Church, who, in October of 1942, declared, *"Motherhood is near to divinity. It is the highest, holiest service to be assumed by mankind. It places her who honors its holy calling and service next to the angels."*[17] No man, conscious of that truth, would *ever* show disrespect to his mother, let alone abuse or neglect her. To do so would be to abuse, neglect, and disrespect the divine. And, no doubt, strict accountability before God would be the consequence.

To *respect* is to give particular attention to and to hold in special or high regard. It is insufficient that a man acknowledges his mother as the source of his life. It is not enough for him to speak of her with warmth. To respect suggests an aspect of doting, of care. The son faithful to this counsel does not simply reverence his mother's name; he sees to her needs and is attentive to the details surrounding her well-being. Just as he feels a divinely appointed mandate to look after his wife and children, he recognizes this same obligation applies to his mother—the one being, after his God, who has been endowed with the power to create life—*his* life!

Elder Matthew Cowley of the Twelve reminded us that mothers are "the co-creators with God of His children." They are endowed with a power akin to God's—a power no mortal man will ever know. Elder Cowley noted that these good women in our lives "belong to the great sorority of saviorhood." They were each "born with an inherent right, an inherent authority to be the saviors of human souls." When faithful to their call to teach, train, nurture, and love, they build testimonies in their children that will guide them throughout their lives and throughout all eternity.[18] We reverence the General Authorities of the Church because of their sacrifices, because of their high and holy calling, and because of the influence they have over us and our testimonies. We, the offspring of our mothers, owe this same respect and reverence to those who bore us because of their sacrifices for us, because of the sacred calling of motherhood, and because they so dramatically affect our testimonies—giving us the foundations we need to successfully traverse this mortal experience.

So much of the mortal experience for practicing Latter-day Saints is learning to align our will with God's. In these verses, the Lord teaches us that in blessing and respecting the women in our lives we actually bless our *own* lives—and align ourselves with God. President David O. McKay testified, "Motherhood is the greatest potential influence either for good or ill in human life."[19] Similarly, President Brigham Young reminded us of the divine reality that what we "imbibe from [our] mothers in infancy, is the most lasting upon the mind through life." Through the teachings of faithful mothers, said Brigham, we each have the potential to develop the "power and faith" had by the two thousand stripling warriors (Alma 56:48).[20] President Joseph F. Smith boldly declared: "If there is any man who ought to merit the curse of Almighty God it is the man who neglects the mother of his child, the wife of his bosom, the one who has made sacrifice of her very life, over and over again for him and his children."[21] When Jehovah revealed from on high the foundational laws we call the Ten Commandments, He commanded all—young and old, male and female—to "honour thy . . . mother: that thy days may be long upon the land which the Lord thy God giveth thee" (Exodus 20:12, Mosiah 13:20). The key as to why honoring one's mother will prolong one's days upon the land may be found in both the symbolism of Jehovah's words and in the verses under consideration in this chapter. This earth is to become the celestial kingdom—our eternal, heavenly abode. As we honor our mothers, we have the promise of a long inheritance upon this globe; not necessarily a long mortal life, but an eternal life upon this exalted earth. In addition, Jesus promised that if we each treat the women in our lives with love and respect, He will grant us "favor in [His] sight" and "many sins shall be forgiven" us! Could there be a greater promise?

Counsel to Women

While much of the counsel above applies to daughters as well as to sons, it seems evident from the verse under inspection that Christ's invitation to men is to respect mothers, and His invitation to women is to be worthy of that respect. Thus, in the aforementioned 1942 statement by the First Presidency, they added this admonition: "To you mothers and mothers-to-be we say: Be chaste, keep pure, live righteously, that your posterity to the last generation may call you blessed."[22] A mother worthy of respect is one who does not live a double standard. The principles she teaches her children are the principles she lives. Thus, President Heber C. Kimball declared: "How pure and angelic females *ought to be* who are sent here to bear the souls of men."[23]

Part of Christ's command in this verse is that those *capable* of being mothers also be *willing* to be such. President James E. Faust stated,

Disturbing is the shift in attitude about the purpose of marriage. More and more young people view marriage "as a couple's relationship, designed to fulfill the emotional needs of adults, rather than an institution for bringing up children." The pursuit of such "soul-mate relationship[s] may [well] weaken marriage as an institution for rearing children." Another disturbing challenge to the family is that children are becoming less valued.[24]

The Church will not dictate how many children to have nor when you should have them, but the Lord's servants have repeatedly called for an attitude of selflessness when it comes to having a family. We must be willing to sacrifice some personal desires and comforts to bring life into this world, and we must be willing to sacrifice some personal goals and accomplishments to rear and nurture our children. As President Ezra Taft Benson reminded us, "in the eternal perspective, children—not possessions, not position, not prestige—are our greatest jewels."[25] The Lord invites us to both have children and to "bring them up in the nurture and admonition of the Lord" (Ephesians 6:4). The work of motherhood is to lead children to keep their second estate.[26] The fulfillment of that divine mandate requires both sacrifice and a willingness to put our children before our own personal desires and goals. As President David O. McKay stressed, "the preservation of self cannot be called noble." He added, "The noblest calling in life, then, must be one in which the attribute of love will manifest itself not for self, but for others."[27] A mother who is second only to God in the eyes of her children will be such because, like God, she lives to nurture and bless her offspring.

VERSE ELEVEN

On her depends the whole existence of man,
for she is his natural and moral support.

The Summary of the Sermon

Men and mankind all exist because of women. That in itself demands our respect. In a world that has for millennia downplayed the contributions of women and oftentimes treated them as second-class citizens, we are reminded of the words of the Apostle Paul: "It is true that the first woman came from a man, but all other men have been given birth by women" (1 Corinthians 11:12, Contemporary English Version). We are dependent beings—every one of us! And ingratitude for our mothers, who have given us life, is a shabby failing!

Like a child who ungratefully takes from his parents without ever expressing gratitude, too often we humans forget the debt we owe to our mothers. They give us physical life, and then most spend the remainder of their days trying to fill us with spiritual life—teaching us morals, spirituality, faith, and obedience. Till their last breath, they emotionally support us because of the nurturing spirit that resides within their souls.

Counsel to Men & Children

The earnest man, if he willingly takes the time to contemplate, will realize that so much of who he is stems from the nurturing, love, and teaching of his mother. Former General Relief Society President Julie B. Beck testified, "Righteous women have changed the course of history and will continue to do so, and their influence will spread and grow exponentially throughout the eternities."[28] What prophet has not been the product of a good and faith-filled mother who instilled in him from his youth a belief and trust in the God of Heaven? Such is the case for many of us. Though I was not reared in a Latter-day Saint home, my good mother taught me to pray, took me to church, and (in her own way) bore fervent witness of her belief that there was a God in heaven to whom I owed respect and obedience. The "whole existence" of every man—including significant elements of his personality, faith, and character—is most often developed at the knee of his mother. This is a debt none of us can repay. Yet it is a debt we must do all we can to acknowledge and honor.

Not only do our mothers give us mortal life, they then physically support us until we become independent beings—feeding, clothing, aiding, and assisting us every single day for years. Each of us is quite literally the product of our mothers. They are our "natural," or physical, and "moral," or spiritual, support in the most developmentally important stage of our lives.

Counsel to Women

In the *The Family: A Proclamation to the World*, it states that "mothers are primarily responsible for the nurture of their children." Echoing this, Elder M. Russell Ballard counseled,

> I am impressed by countless mothers who have learned how important it is to focus on the things that can only be done in a particular season of life. If a child lives with parents for 18 or 19 years, that span is only one-fourth of a parent's life. And the most formative time of all, the early years in a child's life, represents less than one-tenth of a parent's normal life. It is crucial to focus on our children for the short time we have them with us and to seek, with the help of the Lord, to teach them all we can before they leave our homes.[29]

Today we live in a society that tells women that they shouldn't have to make such sacrifices—that daycare is as good as home care for their children. A number of years ago, while teaching a religion class to Stanford University students, a young Latter-day Saint sister—her head filled with the big ideas of a major university—said, "Sociologists have proven that children are better off if they're put in daycare at a young age rather than being reared by their mothers. They are more socially adjusted if someone else raises them." My simple response was this: "Sister, the Lord says you're wrong!" When the Lord has commanded the women of the Church to bear children, in the same breath He commanded that mothers be willing to be their offspring's "natural and moral support." This implies that mothers must be willing to give life, but also to care for their children, to teach them faith and morals, obedience to the commandments, and service to their fellow men.

If a mother is not the source of her child's ethics, values, and faith, who will be? As President Brigham Young taught, the good mothers do "follow [their children] to all eternity."[30]

VERSE TWELVE

She gives birth to you in the midst of suffering.
By the sweat of her brow she rears you,
and until her death you cause her the gravest anxieties.
Bless her and adore her,
for she is your only true friend and support on earth.

The Summary of the Sermon

For most women, pregnancy is quite literally a near-death experience. Were it not for the miracles of modern medicine, out of the five children my wife delivered, three would have died in childbirth, and my wife would have lost her life in two of the pregnancies. Truly, during a pregnancy and delivery a woman walks "through the valley of the shadow of death" (Psalm 23:4). It is a godlike offering that each mother makes!

Those who have reared children know that amid all the joy that comes, there is much sorrow and anxiety. Indeed, as joyous as it is to have children, it is perhaps one of the most straining and draining of mortal experiences. Disappointments are common, and worry never ends.

Yet, as our passage testifies, of all humans, Mother is the one you can most readily trust to love you unconditionally and support you enduringly. Thus the Lord extols her virtues and condemns our lack of adoration.

Counsel to Men & Children

Noticing the myriad small things your mother has done for you is evidence of a grateful soul. Expressing appreciation to your mother for those things is your responsibility as a true follower of Christ. President J. Reuben Clark Jr. taught, "The truest, the holiest thing we know in our whole mortal existence is the mother's love; and its depth, its wisdom, its sympathy, its forgiveness, its hope, its belief, its compassion and faith, are the nearest the divine that we can know here."[31] For all they do and all they endure, mothers deserve to be adored—and that is the command of Christ to all sons and daughters. I like Webster's definition of *adore*: to "honor as a deity or as divine." God dotes upon His children, constantly attending to their most minute needs. Only a mother can compare! And like God's blessings to us, which so often go unnoticed, we are each the recipient of more blessings than we know from our mothers. Thank them!

Counsel to Women

The supportive and optimistic nature of mothers and wives is encapsulated by the following words from Elder Russell M. Nelson: "Thank the Lord for these sisters who—like our Heavenly Father—love us not only for what we are but for what we may become."[32] Good and inspired mothers and wives can see the diamond in the rough! They don't dwell upon the flaws in their children or husbands. Rather, they look for the good—for that which they can praise. And they are ever hopeful that he whom they bore, or he whom they married, will become all his God-given endowments have foreordained him to become.

While she sacrifices to give us life, and then patiently endures while we attempt to develop into contributing humans, there is something else that the Latter-day Saint mother does that blesses and equips her children to make it through this life relatively unscathed: live the gospel. It is that simple. Live the gospel! President Joseph F. Smith remarked,

> I learned in my childhood, as most children, probably, have learned . . . that no love in all the world can equal the love of a true mother. . . . I have sometimes felt, how could even the Father love his children more than my mother loved her children? . . . Whenever [temptations] became most alluring and most tempting to me, the first thought that arose in my soul was this: Remember the love of your mother. I have learned to place a high estimate on the love of a mother. I have often said, and I will repeat it, that the love of a true mother comes nearer being like the love of God than any other kind of love.[33]

The mother who faithfully lives the gospel becomes a source of strength to her offspring because, in their hour of temptation, thoughts of her can insulate them from the powerful temptations of this world.

Of the tremendous effort that it takes to be the kind of mother our verse describes, Elder M. Russell Ballard said:

We need to remember that the full commitment of motherhood and of putting children first can be difficult. . . . There are moments of great joy and incredible fulfillment, but there are also moments of a sense of inadequacy, monotony, and frustration. Mothers may feel they receive little or no appreciation for the choice they have made. Sometimes even husbands seem to have no idea of the demands upon their wives. As a Church, we have enormous respect and gratitude to you mothers of young children.

Elder Ballard then added that the names of faithful mothers "are recorded in the Lamb's book of life." Knowing that, they should:

Continue to go forward. Go forward in faith and humility. Do not let Satan or any of his seductive evil power have influence over you. Give no occasion to the adversary nor allow him to diminish your God-given, unique sensitivity to the Spirit of the Lord. May that Spirit ever guide you to sacred feelings in your every thought and activity as you reach out to others in love and mercy.[34]

Similarly, Sister Ruth H. Funk, former general president of the Young Women's organization, taught, "Our only peace, through disappointments, sorrow, and challenges, will come as we draw nearer unto him. With such love for our Redeemer, every difficult experience may be met with courage, acceptance, and even gratitude. His love for us is a gift beyond price. What does he ask in return? 'Love one another; as I have loved you' (John 13:34)."[35]

VERSE FOURTEEN

In the same way, love your wives and respect them;
for they will be mothers tomorrow,
and each later on the ancestress of a race.

The Summary of the Sermon

While much of Christ's discourse to this point has been applicable to children and adults, sons and daughters, here the Lord directs His words—His commands—to married men.

As would be expected, Jesus continues to extol women. But now He speaks of the eternal implications of marriage—and the role of women therein.

The Lord introduces into His discourse the sacred doctrine of deification. He indicates that, through the Abrahamic covenant, each faithful woman will be blessed to be the mother of children—ideally in time, but certainly in eternity. And He reminds His hearers that every woman who is sealed in the new and everlasting covenant of marriage will be "the ancestress of a race." She is destined, through Christ and her faithfulness to Him, to be a queen and priestess—a goddess—throughout all eternity!

Knowing this truth and understanding that this divinely revealed principle is foundational to the Lord's great plan of happiness, each man must love, cherish, and praise his wife and teach their promised posterity to do the same.

Counsel to Men & Children

With emotion in his voice, President Joseph F. Smith begged the men of the Church: "Oh! my brethren, be true to your families, be true to your wives and to your children."[36] Being true to wives and children means more than basic fidelity. It includes being true to the command to show one's spouse love, adoration, and respect, but it also requires that we teach our children to feel and act this same way toward their mothers and grandmothers. The Apostle Paul taught,

> Husbands, love your wives, even as Christ also loved the church, and gave himself for it. . . . So ought men to love their wives as their own bodies. He that loveth his wife loveth himself. For no man ever yet hated his own flesh; but nourisheth and cherisheth it, even as the Lord the church: For we are members of his body, of his flesh, and of his bones. For this cause shall a man leave his father and mother, and shall be joined unto his wife, and they two shall be one flesh. This is a great mystery: but I speak concerning Christ and the church. Nevertheless let every one of you in particular so love his wife even as himself; and the wife [see] that she reverence [her] husband. (Ephesians 5:25, 28–33)

Paul's command is no small request. He invites men to feel toward their wives what the Lord would feel toward them. Such a love and commitment could never be developed

though a casual approach to marriage. Indeed, a love that deep
and encompassing would require of any man fervent prayer,
continual sacrifice, and a consistent vigilance to his wife's righteous desires and needs. Paul is ultimately inviting us to become
what each of us are commanded to become—true and abiding
Christians. For the men, he suggests that this might well be
accomplished by nurturing our relationship with our wives.
If a man develops, through the enabling power of Christ, the
ability to see his wife as Paul says he should, he will then sense
the truth of President Smith's declaration that "motherhood
lies at the foundation of happiness in the home."[37]

Counsel to Women

Importantly, for those who suffer because of the emotional
pains that come from infertility, Christ here offers hope and
eternal perspective. Every faithful woman will bear offspring.
None will be robbed of the blessing of motherhood. This blessing must come on the Lord's timetable, but it *will* come. Elder
Joseph B. Wirthlin reminded us: "The Lord compensates the
faithful for every loss. That which is taken away from those
who love the Lord will be added unto them in His own way.
While it may not come at the time we desire, the faithful will
know that every tear today will eventually be returned a hun-
dredfold with tears of rejoicing and gratitude."[38] In the verse
under consideration, Christ promises fertility to the infertile
and blessings to those who have yet to be blessed.

In this fourteenth verse of Christ's discourse on the sacred
place of women, Jesus reminds men that women have the
potential to become goddesses. However, we must not forget

that the implication of that truth is that women must live up to this divine calling. Though thankfully infrequent, there is the occasional sister who demands to be treated like a god but then acts like a devil. The Lord praises the women of the Church and extols their divine destiny because so many naturally live up to this divine destiny. Just as Christ calls the men to introspection in how they treat the women in their lives, by default He is also calling the women to self-examination regarding their worthiness to be treated as goddesses. President James E. Faust once noted: "I fear you sisters do not realize in the smallest part the extent of your influence for good in your families, in the Church, and in society. Your influence for good is incalculable and indescribable." He added, "I truly believe you are instruments in the hands of God in your many roles. . . . Sacred blessings and righteous influence have flowed into my own life and my family's lives from my beloved wife, her mother, my own mother, grandmothers, my precious daughters, and granddaughters."[39] President Faust was blessed by the influence of good, righteous, kind, and loving women in his life. The Lord calls all women to seek that ideal and to treat those within their stewardship in a kind, loving, and Christian way.

VERSES FIFTEEN & SEVENTEEN

Be submissive toward your wife.
Her love ennobles man, softens his hardened heart,
tames the brute in him, and makes of him a lamb.
Even as the God of hosts separated of old
the light from the darkness
and the land from the waters, woman possesses the divine talent
of separating in a man good intentions from evil thoughts.

The Summary of the Sermon

Elder Bruce R. McConkie penned these wise words of counsel: "The most important things that any member of The Church of Jesus Christ of Latter-day Saints ever does in this world are: 1. To marry the right person, in the right place, by the right authority; and 2. To keep the covenant made in connection with this holy and perfect order of matrimony."[40] Likewise, Elder Russell M. Nelson taught:

> To you who are not yet married, think about your future marriage. Choose your companion well. Remember the scriptures that teach the importance of marriage in the temple:

"In the celestial glory there are three heavens or degrees; And in order to obtain the highest, a man must enter into this order of the priesthood [meaning the new and everlasting covenant of marriage]; And if he does not, he cannot obtain it." The highest ordinances in the house of the Lord are received by husband and wife together and equally—or not at all![41]

Clearly, marriage has eternal implications. And as more than half of all marriages end in divorce, the influence of a spouse—for good or ill—cannot be denied. One must choose wisely!

In these verses Jesus declares the power women have over men in helping them along the path toward God and godhood. A Christlike wife can elevate her husband and his desires. She can soften his heart, tame whatever is rebellious or hard in him, and make him more like the Lamb of God. Good women have the power to change a natural man into a godly man. Jesus so declares it.

Counsel to Men

Jesus's primary counsel to men in this verse is that they be submissive to their wives. Lest this be taken out of context to imply that men should no longer lead out in the home or that women should act in a domineering and demanding way, allow me to clarify. The Lord, through His chosen servants, has said much about the native spiritual gifts of women and how those gifts can bless their families and their marriages when exercised in righteousness and love. For example, President Ezra Taft Benson taught, "A woman's role in a man's life is to lift him, to help him."[42] Elder McConkie taught, "Women are appointed . . . to be guides and lights in righteousness in the family unit, and to engineer and arrange so that things are done in the way that will result in the salvation of more of our Father's children."[43] President Harold B. Lee reminded men that, without the support of a devoted wife, "no man can hold a position in this church and hope to continue to serve as he has been called."[44] Elder Vaughn J. Featherstone of the Seventy noted: "Women are endowed with special traits and attributes that come trailing down through eternity from a divine mother. Young women have special God-given feelings about charity, love, and obedience. Coarseness and vulgarity are contrary to their natures. They have a modifying, softening influence on young men."[45] Similarly, President Brigham Young said that when women "carry out the instincts of their nature, they . . . effect a revolution for good."[46]

What Jesus was counseling in our verse at hand and what the Lord's prophets have confirmed is this: men should respect and give heed to the spiritual promptings of their wives, including promptings or counsel regarding how to become more like Christ. And, just as no spiritually in-tune woman would be bothered by the command to "submit" (Ephesians 5:22–25) to a husband who is faithfully keeping the commandments and honoring his priesthood, so also a righteous man who is seeking his own salvation and that of his family should not be bothered by Christ's command here to "be submissive toward your wife" when she offers good, inspired counsel—particularly when such is offered in a spirit of love and aid.

Counsel to Women

The Apostle Paul declared: "And the woman which hath an husband that believeth not, and if he be pleased to dwell with her, let her not leave him. For the unbelieving husband is sanctified by the wife. . . . For what knowest thou, O wife, whether thou shalt save thy husband?" (1 Corinthians 7:13–15). Paul's point was that women can have a salvific influence upon their husbands. Of course, his advice has application beyond the nonmember spouse. The husband who "believeth not" in family prayer can be sanctified by a patient, faithful, and loving wife, as can be the husband who "believeth not" in family home evening, leading out in the home, paying tithing, keeping the Sabbath day holy, and so on. Rather than giving up on him, Paul encourages the woman of faith to tenderly bless and encourage him. As President Monson said to the sisters of the Church, "If we are observant and aware, and if we act on the promptings which come to us, we can accomplish much good."[47]

The call of women is to lift, to inspire, and to save. Elder Matthew Cowley of the Twelve taught, "You sisters belong to the great sorority of saviorhood. . . . You are born with an inherent right, an inherent authority to be the saviors of human souls."[48] Elder Russell M. Nelson taught, "To help another human being reach one's celestial potential is part of the divine mission of women. . . . In partnership with God, her divine mission is to help . . . souls be lifted. This is the measure of her creation. It is ennobling, edifying, and exalting."[49] What a blessing to have such a holy and noble calling—and to be divinely endowed with natural gifts to accomplish it! Hugh B. Brown admonished the women of the Church:

Sisters, don't give up because your men are not all you would wish them to be, but maintain your faith, not only in them but in your Heavenly Father's help and your own ability to fulfill your role as a helpmate. Never cease to work and pray for divine guidance in your divine calling. Thus may you hold your families together and prepare them for the eternities to come.[50]

What a tragedy it is when believing Latter-day Saint women do not realize their God-given gift to change the world and to encourage their husbands toward goodness and faithfulness. From a very young age sisters possess this power, but all too many neglect to nurture it or inappropriately utilize it to manipulate instead of to bless. President Packer explained how this endowment can be used, even by young sisters, for good:

> Some young men are—now I must choose the right word—forced? persuaded? encouraged? compelled? to serve a mission by a sweet girl. She flashes her pretty eyelashes and says with some determination that she will one day marry one who has served an honorable mission. . . . How quickly a young hero will line up to enlist with that kind of encouragement. God bless the sisters who have such power to recruit missionaries.[51]

Sisters, the Lord has called you to ennoble man, to soften his heart, and to tame the brute in him. He has charged you with the responsibility to help your husbands and sons distinguish light from darkness and shun all evil behavior and thoughts. You have been endowed with the spiritual gifts necessary to accomplish this. You must not neglect this responsibility, but you must also recognize the importance of being directed by the Spirit in fulfilling this charge. There is always the risk of being less a tutor and more a nag! President Joseph F. Smith cautioned,

> The wife . . . should treat the husband with the greatest respect and courtesy. Her words to him should not be keen and cutting and sarcastic. She should not pass slurs or insinuations at him. She should not nag him. She should not try to arouse his anger or make things unpleasant about the home. The wife should be a joy to her husband, and she should live and conduct herself at home so the home will be the most joyous, the most blessed place on earth to her husband.[52]

Elder Stephen L. Richards of the Twelve likewise stated, "I always regret seeing a woman do anything to belittle her husband, even for his mistakes."[53] And from President Harold B. Lee we find this: "Wives, may I plead with you to try to understand us, stubborn, strong-willed, sometimes careless, thoughtless men. . . . Keep on saying to us that you understand us, you want to help. . . . Do not let your man say, and say it honestly, 'My wife doesn't appreciate what I do. She doesn't care.'"[54] President Lee added, "If you want a man to become your ideal, you have got to help him to be so."[55] Nagging, of course, is not helping. If you are teaching and encouraging because you want to bless him and your family, then the Lord's Spirit will guide and direct you in what you say and how you say it. If you have selfish motivations in your corrective counsel, you will not have the aid of the Holy Ghost.

Finally, President Lee pointed out that faithful Latter-day Saint women are wives first and mothers second. He noted, "her role as a wife has priority."[56] As she nurtures the relationship with her husband, she has the ability to tame the brute in him and thereby bless the children. The sealing between a husband and wife is imperative for their eternal work, and yet, too many focus on their children (who will eventually have their own eternal companions) while neglecting their relationship with their spouse. If the marriage is healthy, the family will be healthy. This is not a commission to neglect one's children. It is a call to place first things first. As President Lee stated, "A woman happy with her husband is better for her children than a hundred books on child welfare."[57] He went on to say, "One of the greatest enemies of happiness in the home is the word *apathy*; to fail to take interest or concern or to share can begin to erode until finally the house can collapse."[58]

VERSE SIXTEEN

*The wife and the mother are the inappreciable
treasures given unto you by God.
They are the fairest ornaments of existence,
and of them shall be born all the inhabitants of the world.*

The Summary of the Sermon

The women in our lives—whether they be our wives, mothers, sisters, or daughters—are gifts from God. They are to be treasured, the Lord tells us. Yet, we are informed, so often their goodness and sacred contributions go unperceived by us.

Christ speaks of them as "fair"—as "ornaments of existence"—implying not only their innate beauty, but also their God-given gift for creating beauty in our homes and in our lives.

Jesus reminds each of us that women have a divine gift—that of creating life. In this they are like God and unlike man, who has not been endowed with so godlike a gift!

Counsel to Men

A man who treats poorly his wife, mother, or any other woman makes a loud, declarative statement about his true feelings toward the "fairer sex." On many occasions, President Gordon B. Hinckley made comments akin to this one:

> Treat your wives with kindness. One of the great sorrows of this world which has been among people for generations in all lands has been the abuse of wives. No man is worthy of the priesthood who abuses his wife, the mother of his children. Extend to her your love, your respect, your appreciation. You cannot enter the highest degree of glory in the kingdom of heaven unless you go there walking hand in hand with your companion at your side. The Lord has made that clear.[59]

President Hinckley informed the women of the Church, "We walk at your side as your companions and your brethren with respect and love, with honor and great admiration."[60] This was not simply an assertion—it was a promise. And the prophet made it clear on many occasions how adamant he was about this. No man could be worthy to hold the priesthood of God who consciously treated his wife, mother, daughter, or any other woman with disrespect or degradation. Christ's command is that we treat the women in our lives as "treasures"—to be protected, valued, prized, and adored. The Savior elsewhere warned us, "For it is not meet that . . . the pearls . . . be cast before swine" (D&C 41:6). In verse sixteen of Christ's discourse on the sacred place of women, he declares that females are pearls to be treasured. Should we, as men, trample them as would swine, we should expect to lose them in the eternities—along with our salvation.

While physical beauty may only be skin deep, the beauty of the soul of a faithful Latter-day Saint woman is all-encompassing. They beautify the lives of their husbands because they often have a gift for beautifying their surroundings. Through them is born every "inhabitant of the world," and thus they beautify the life of their husbands by giving them children—beautiful children! So much of the aesthetically pleasing things of this life are created by the women who raise us, who love us, and who serve us.

As "the ancestress of a race" (verse 14), women have been endowed with a divine power unique to God—the power to create life. Elder Vaughn J. Featherstone of the Seventy pointed out,

> Young women were not foreordained to do what priesthood holders do. Theirs is a sacred, God-given role, and the traits they received from heavenly mother are equally as important as those given to the young men. Sometimes misguided women or men direct our youth away from their divinely appointed role. Worlds without end, men will never be able to bear children. Every young woman may be a procreator with God and carry a little one under her breast either in this life or in the eternal worlds. Motherhood is a wonderful, priceless blessing, no matter what all the world may say.[61]

Knowing this, how can any man feel anything but awe for the women in his life? If we treasure our God, we necessarily must treasure the women who walk the path of life by our sides—those who have given us life, who give us children, and who are born to us as our dear daughters.

Counsel to Women

When God promised us that we could become like Him, He did not say that we would do so unconditionally. Rather, He offered us blessings—gifts—that were attainable and that, if pursued, would bring us great joy in this life and incomprehensible happiness in the life to come. In the verse under examination, the Lord speaks of wives and mothers as "inappreciable treasures" who are to be a gift from God to their husbands and sons. Sometimes women are unrecognizable as treasures because the men in their lives are inattentive or ungrateful. Sometimes, however, they are inappreciable as treasure because they choose to do so little for their husbands or sons that they manifest no treasurable attributes. One would hope this to be a rare circumstance in the Church, though in years of counseling with married couples, I have found it to be more common than any of us would wish to believe. It is one thing to be loved, but it is quite another to be lovable. It is one thing to want to be treasured, but it is another thing to act in such a way as to provoke the awe and adoration desired. Here the Lord instructs men to treasure their wives and mothers. But, by default, He also commands women to act in a treasurable manner—to be loving, warm, nurturing, and Christlike. He surely would condemn nagging, criticism, ingratitude, harshness, emotional coldness, or any other unkind behavior or attribute that would harm a relationship. One of the best ways to be treasured is to seek to be treasurable—even amid those trying times that come to all families and all relationships.

The Lord speaks of the beauty of women. Of course, there is no right look or right weight, no better nose or better body.

For each of us there is someone to love and someone to be loved by. And whether that person is discovered here in time or only in eternity, we have the promise of the Lord that, if we are faithful to our covenants, we will find our eternal companion. But we also must exercise our agency to find our everlasting mate—and to live in such a way after marriage that our companion desires to be with us throughout eternity. Elder Richard G. Scott told of a man he once met, who well illustrates this point:

> His first comment to me was, "Why doesn't the Lord give me a wife?" as though an eternal companion were a teddy bear to be acquired with no thought of her agency. As we spoke, it was obvious he was not doing the most fundamental things to qualify to find a wife. He admitted that maybe he should do something about his excessive weight, but that was hard. His clothes were slovenly and his body so neglected that it was difficult to stand near him. Clearly, he is not doing his part.[62]

This is in no way an indictment of those who struggle with weight issues or with a less-than-attractive figure or face. These are not the things that make a marriage happy or unhappy, nor are they what will matter in the eternities. But I have known a woman or two who would gladly get dolled up to go out but would do little to beautify themselves while at home— who would clean house for visitors, but otherwise allow their families to live in relative squalor. Christ's declaration about the beauty of women is also an invitation for them to create beauty—to beautify themselves and their surroundings. Such acts should be accomplished as much for their children and spouse as for any guest or acquaintance. As one commentator on relationships noted, "It would be a stunner for" some women "to realize that they try harder to impress strangers than they try to impress the person who is supposed to be the most important to them."[63] To fix themselves up for those who are *not* part of their family but to let themselves (or their home) go for those they are supposed to love the most sends a strong message about who they really love. It is a contradiction to Christ's description of what His daughters should seek to be. As President Gordon B. Hinckley noted, "Of all the creations of the Almighty, there is none more beautiful, none more inspiring than a lovely daughter of God who walks in virtue."[64] He also said,

> In the pioneering days of this church when men grubbed the sagebrush and broke the sod so that crops might be planted to sustain life, many a wife and mother planted a few flowers and a few fruit trees to add beauty and taste to the drabness of pioneer life. There are so many things that you can do. Beauty is a thing divine. The cultivation of it becomes an expression of the divine nature within you.[65]

The Lord calls women to create beauty in the world because that is what God would do and because God has endowed each sister with the gifts necessary to be able to create beauty in her own wonderful way.

Finally, in verse sixteen the Lord speaks of women in their divine roles of mother and matriarch. While, sadly, some cannot bear children in this life, nevertheless, the faithful are promised that they *will* have children, if not in time then in eternity. But this promise is also a command: "Be fruitful, and multiply, and replenish the earth" (Genesis 1:28). The Church does not tell women when to have children or how many they should have, but certainly the eternal callings of mother and matriarch bless those who earnestly seek to fulfill the Lord's command to multiply according to the personal dictates of the Holy Spirit. Of course, this is not simply a call to give birth but also to love, care for, and bring up children "in the nurture and admonition of the Lord" (Enos 1:1). As *The Family: A Proclamation to the World* states,

> Husband and wife have a solemn responsibility to love and care for each other and for their children. "Children are an heritage of the Lord" (Psalm 127:3). Parents have a sacred duty to rear their children in love and righteousness, to provide for their physical and spiritual needs, and to teach them to love and serve one another, observe the commandments of God, and be law-abiding citizens wherever they live. Husbands and wives—mothers and fathers—will be held accountable before God for the discharge of these obligations. . . . Mothers are primarily responsible for the nurture of their children.[66]

We are living in a world where fewer and fewer people are willing to give birth to children or make the sacrifices necessary to personally rear them once they are born. Husbands and wives, mothers and fathers, are to share in this sacred responsibility. Neither can abdicate this without incurring accountability before God. Said President Brigham Young, "There are multitudes of pure and holy spirits waiting to take tabernacles, now what is our duty?—To prepare tabernacles for them; to take a course that will not tend to drive those spirits into the families of the wicked, where they will be trained in wickedness, debauchery, and every species of crime."[67] For all the inhabitants of the world to be born, each woman of Zion must be willing to embrace her role and calling as mother and matriarch—the rest of the world has largely rejected it.

VERSE EIGHTEEN

Wherefore I say unto you, after God
your best thoughts should belong to women and to wives,
woman being for you the temple wherein you will
most easily obtain perfect happiness.

The Summary of the Sermon

The psalmist declared, "Search me, O God, and know my heart: try me, and know my thoughts" (Psalm 139:23). Certainly the Lord does know all that we think and feel, both of Him and of our fellow beings. Thus, King Benjamin warned:

> But this much I can tell you, that if ye do not watch yourselves, and your thoughts, and your words, and your deeds, and observe the commandments of God, and continue in the faith of what ye have heard concerning the coming of our Lord, even unto the end of your lives, ye must perish. And now, O man, remember, and perish not. (Mosiah 4:30)

In verse 18 of Christ's discourse, we are told that men's greatest and highest thoughts should be for God. But second only to those elevating thoughts of divinity should be heartening feelings and thoughts about women—particularly their wives. He reminds His male hearers that in and through their wives they will find "perfect happiness," and this because, in the words of the Lord, righteous, kind, and loving wives are "temples" of "perfect happiness."

Counsel to Men

These are trying times—in more ways than one. As we have already noted, divorces are on the rise nationally. Even within the Church, we see more and more Latter-day Saints who were sealed for time and all eternity in the Lord's holy temple grow apart and lose their love for one another. Though there are circumstances in which divorce may be necessary and even best, these cases should be the exception, not the rule. President Ezra Taft Benson wisely noted, "Husbands and wives who love each other will find that love and loyalty are reciprocated. This love will provide a nurturing atmosphere for the emotional growth of children. Family life should be a time of happiness and joy that children can look back on with fond memories and associations."[68] President Benson's comment about the reciprocating nature of love and loyalty are but an echo of Christ's declaration that men should manifest high regard for their wives and, in sincerely doing, know that these godly women will reciprocate by being the temples in which these loving husbands "will most easily obtain perfect happiness." Of course, the man's role is to *sincerely* and *truly* see their wives in this divine way and to manifest that in their words and actions. Men should think of their wives much as President Hinckley described them: "As His final creation, the crowning event of His glorious work," God "created woman. I like to regard Eve as His masterpiece . . . the final work before He rested from His labors. I do not regard her as being in second place to Adam."[69] The Lord commanded husbands, "Thou shalt love thy wife with all thy heart" (D&C 42:22). President Lorenzo Snow expressed concern to the men of the Church, saying that some of you "do not value your wives as you should." He added this counsel: "Be kind to them. . . . Be kind when sometimes you have to make a little sacrifice to do so; feel kind anyway, no matter what the sacrifice."[70] The only men who find their wives "temples of perfect happiness" are those who truly adore their eternal companions with all of their hearts.

Counsel to Women

President Brigham Young once suggested, "I doubt whether it can be found, from the revelations that are given and the facts as they exist, that there is a female in all the regions of hell."[71] Of course, President Young was speaking in hyperbole, but what a glorious thing it would be if all wives lived so as to insure the truthfulness of the prophet's pronouncement. Elder Joseph A. Merrill of the Twelve once noted: "A Latter-day Saint marriage is a union of two equal partners, obligated to build a home where mutual love, respect, trust, fidelity, tolerance, patience, and kindness are some of the essential operating factors. And in the home where these prevail the ugly specter of divorce will never enter."[72] As a wife, are you worthy of thoughts so aggrandizing as to place you second only to God? Do you seek to be "the temple wherein" your husband "will most easily obtain perfect happiness"? The temple is a place of safety, security, peace, and love. Are you that to your husband? If not, what might you change in order to be worthy of the title "temple of perfect happiness"? Marital problems are seldom the fault of just one partner. Nevertheless, too many say to themselves, "When my spouse starts doing such and such, then I'll meet his needs!" Such an attitude is both selfish and destructive. Men and women are called to be selfless partners in a marriage. We are each called to sacrifice for our spouse as Christ sacrificed for the Church (Ephesians 5). In verse 18 of His discourse on women, Jesus does not extol men. Rather, He exalts women, and by implication extends an invitation to them to be as He describes them—temples of happiness! Women, more than men, set the tone in a home and determine the spirit of the home. Creating a home that feels like a temple requires first creating a marriage that feels like one. The Lord here invites His female hearers to contemplate how they might more readily do that.

VERSE NINETEEN

*Here [through the women in your life] you will
forget your sorrows and your failures,
and you will recover the lost energy necessary
to enable you to help your neighbor.*

The Summary of the Sermon

The best of lives still encounter opposition, failure, and their accompanying sorrows. But through the love and interaction of a good wife or mother, a boy or man can overcome these trials, finding strength and meaning in his disappointment and recovering lost motivation to do good. He can, through her, rediscover the godly qualities so often tempered by the harsh world we live in.

Counsel to Men & Children

It strikes me as curious that in scripture God is often associated with feminine attributes. As one commentator noted, "There is a feminine face of God in the Hebrew Scriptures—images and metaphors for God and God's activities that are drawn from the world of women's experience."[73] For example, the Hebrew word we would traditionally translate in English as God's *mercy* or *compassion* means literally "womb love." In Isaiah 49:15 God is depicted as a nursing mother. In Deuteronomy 32:11–12 He is portrayed as a mother eagle teaching, protecting, and supporting her children. In Hosea 13:8 God describes divine love as being like what a mother bear feels for her young cubs—including a willingness to do anything to protect her children. Curiously, in Matthew 23:37 Jesus uses feminine language to describe the type of love that God and Christ have for those who profess a belief in them—saying it is like the love of a mother hen who gathers her chicks under her wings to protect them. These connections between God and Christ and things feminine should not be lost on the reader. The Lord's prophets seem to be emphasizing the divine nature of certain attributes—attributes largely associated with women. Christ can promise men that in their wives and mothers they will find comfort from their sorrows and their failures because women, generally speaking, are naturally endowed with a compassionate and nurturing spirit. This makes them instruments in God's hands and enables them to be a blessing to their children and husbands.

Here the Lord reminds men of this gift common among women and encourages His sons, in their dark hours, to turn to the wives and mothers in their lives. In a man's hour of desperation or despair, a good woman can often help him to see things "as they really are" (Jacob 4:13). That gift—that blessing—can both lift his spirits and help him recover any lost motivation to do as God and Christ would do in the world, at work, at Church, and in the home. A wise man knows this and takes advantage of the blessing it is to have a wife, mother, or sister with whom he can counsel and wherein he can find support. President Joseph Fielding Smith wrote,

> The Lord said he would give the man a companion who would be a help meet for him: that is, a help who would answer all the requirements, not only of companionship, but also through whom the fullness of the purposes of the Lord could be accomplished regarding the mission of man through mortal life and into eternity.[74]

Women are exactly that! They are the perfect "help meets" to the men in their lives. Traditionally the title *help meet* (seen in Genesis 2:18) is understood to mean "a helper fit for him,"[75] "a helper like-the-opposite-of-him,"[76] or "a help corresponding to him."[77] In other words, it suggests an equal but opposite half of the whole. It does not, as some have supposed, mean a servant-helper or an inferior.[78] Thus the ideal relationship, as depicted in Eden consists of man and woman—husband and wife—being perfectly one: two halves of the same whole. In the third century AD, one early Christian father noted that God provided Adam with Eve because He knew what a blessing woman would be to man and to the Church.[79] More recently, one commentator penned the following: "He who has a good God, a good heart, and a good wife, to converse with, and yet complains he lacks conversation, would not have been easy and content in paradise."[80] The Lord has given man woman so that he has, during this difficult mortal journey, an ideal and divinely inspired helper. Praised be the Father for this wonderful (but tragically undervalued and underutilized) gift!

Counsel to Women

President George Albert Smith noted, "Whenever there was a great leader in Israel there was a great wife or mother or both who stood by his side."[81] Helaman's two thousand stripling warriors epitomize this truth. "They had been taught by their mothers, that if they did not doubt, God would deliver them. And they rehearsed . . . the words of their mothers, saying: We do not doubt our mothers knew it" (Alma 56:47–48). Such is the influence of a good woman upon her sons and husband. Such is the call and commission of every Latter-day Saint woman. She builds faith, overcomes fears, comforts in times of doubt, sorrow, failure, or fear, and lovingly motivates the men in her life to reach for higher things. On the backs of such women rests the success of the kingdom of God. On their shoulders stand the successful leaders of the Church.

VERSE TWENTY

Do not expose her to humiliation.
In acting thus you would humiliate yourselves
and lose the sentiment of love,
without which nothing exists here upon earth.

The Summary of the Sermon:

In counseling the Nephite men—largely members of his own family—Jacob, the brother of Nephi, reprovingly stated,

> Behold, ye have done greater iniquities than the Lamanites, our brethren. Ye have broken the hearts of your tender wives, and lost the confidence of your children, because of your bad examples before them; and the sobbings of their hearts ascend up to God against you. And because of the strictness of the word of God, which cometh down against you, many hearts died, pierced with deep wounds. (Jacob 2:35)

Never humiliate or belittle your wife or mother. God will hold men accountable for the way they treat their wives and mothers. There will surely be an accounting for the pain caused to those tender-hearted women who are abused. But there shall also be accountability for setting a bad example for the rising generation who witness the abuse. One can never find justification for the intentional humiliation of another person. Such behavior is the antithesis of love.

Counsel to Men & Children

In verse 20 of His discourse, the Lord informs us that any man who humiliates a woman brings shame and humiliation upon himself. Such acts will surely cost him the love of his wife and, ultimately, the loss of his salvation. Those who dwell in the highest degree of the celestial kingdom are they who have entered into and kept the covenants associated with the new and everlasting covenant of marriage. The Holy Spirit of Promise will not ratify the sealing of a man who demeans or humiliates his companion (D&C 132:7). President Joseph F. Smith counseled the brethren of the priesthood with these words: "The husband should treat his wife with the utmost courtesy and respect. The husband should never insult her; he should never speak slightly of her, but he should always hold her in the highest esteem in the home, [and] in the presence of their children."[82]

Any man who verbally or emotionally abuses his wife, in front of his children or in private, is not worthy of the title *father*. For a young man to witness his father demeaning his mother does irreparable damage to the psyche of that future husband and father. President Lorenzo Snow noted that this is a more common problem in the Church than many would think: "To the husbands I say: Many of you do not value your wives as you should."[83] Elder Stephen L. Richards of the Twelve stated, "I . . . have no sympathy with a husband who would embarrass his wife before her children. . . . I believe as we preserve the integrity of the home as it was meant to be, we will do that which we should for the building up of the kingdom."[84]

Those brethren who struggle with this or any equivalent weakness should immediately seek the help of the Lord and their bishop—for the sake of their marriage, their family, and their salvation.

Counsel to Women

While there is never any valid excuse for a man to humiliate or denigrate a woman, the reverse is also true—no faithful Latter-day Saint woman can truthfully claim she keeps the covenants she made in the temple when she is guilty of berating her husband, criticizing him to others, or treating him with coldness as a punishment for perceived bad behavior on his part. Daughters of God should be cherished by their mates, but they should also cherish their companions. They should seek to be the kind of women no man would ever wish to humiliate. Situational ethics are unbecoming of any member of the Church—male or female. To expect respect but give grief is unfitting of any person who professes to be a follower of the Lord Jesus Christ.

VERSE TWENTY-ONE

Protect your wife,
in order that she may protect you and all your family.
All that you do for your wife, your mother,
for a widow or another woman in distress,
you will have done unto your God.

The Summary of the Sermon

In the eyes of the Lord, men and women are unequivocally equal—though certainly different. Too often we forget that equality and sameness are not equivalent. In *The Family: A Proclamation to the World,* we read:

> By divine design, fathers are to preside over their families in love and righteousness and are responsible to provide the necessities of life and protection for their families. Mothers are primarily responsible for the nurture of their children. In these sacred responsibilities, fathers and mothers are obligated to help one another as equal partners. Disability, death, or other circumstances may necessitate individual adaptation.[85]

Men and women have divinely assigned roles and should support each other in the accomplishment of them. One of the roles of men is to be the protector of his wife and children. As men seek to serve, protect, and provide for their wives, mothers, or children, they are blessed with the assurance that the heavens rejoice, for such service is pleasing unto God.

Counsel to Men & Children

As Eve's act in Eden introduced this telestial, mortal probation, she was sent forth to be tried and tested. However, she was not expected to brave the lone and dreary world alone. God sent with her a help, Adam—he being physically stronger than she—that he might serve as a protector and provider. So also, God has not sent us—the Church—to walk the danger-strewn path of mortality alone. He has sent us a companion in Christ. His strengths far exceed our own. He will serve as our protector and provider throughout this daunting existence so long as we keep His Spirit with us. As Adam served as Eve's protector and provider and as Christ is the protector and provider of all who will accept Him, so also every male in the Church is expected to protect and provide for his wife and children to the best of his ability. As President Joseph F. Smith said, "May the fathers in Israel live as they should live; treat their wives as they should treat them; make their homes as comfortable as they possibly can; lighten the burden upon their companions as much as possible."[86] President Smith added that our wives have sacrificed their very lives over and over again for their husbands and their children. To not acknowledge this or to neglect her merits "the curse of Almighty God."[87]

Just as an adult male is to provide for his wife and children, he has a lifelong responsibility to his parents—particularly his mother. Even in his mature years, he is wise to heed the counsel he received at the knee of his mother when he was but a youth. As the proverb says, "My son . . . forsake not the law of thy mother" (Proverbs 6:20). That being said, a mature man—one of spiritual depth—knows he owes his mother more than token obedience to her counsel. Another proverb states, "A foolish man despiseth his mother" (Proverbs 15:20). Elsewhere we read, "Despise not thy mother when she is old" (Proverbs 23:22). A man's responsibility to his mother never ends. The woman who gave him life deserves his attention until she leaves this life—regardless of the sacrifice it requires of him.

In this concluding verse of Jesus's discourse on the sacred place of women, He states, "All that you do for your wife, your mother, for a widow or another woman in distress, you will have done unto your God." Elsewhere Jesus taught, "Inasmuch as ye have done it unto one of the least of these my brethren, ye have done it unto me" (Matthew 25:40). King Benjamin similarly instructed his people, "when ye are in the service of your fellow beings ye are only in the service of your God" (Mosiah 2:17). How a man treats his wife or mother is ultimately a statement about how he loves and would treat his God—a sobering reality.[88]

Counsel to Women

The Lord counseled the men of the Church to "Protect your wife . . . that she may protect you and all your family." The woman's primary role is not to be a physical protector, but rather a protector of that which is sacred—the sanctity of the family, the sacredness of the home, and the testimonies of the children. Because she is typically the one who is most often present during the nurturing years, she insures that the home is a spiritual haven from the world and its influence. In this, husband and wife are partners, but her influence is more evident. Just as the Lord commands men to be physical protectors, He commands women to protect that which falls under their stewardship. To abdicate this by choice is a sin.

In order for a wife, mother, or any sister in the Church to have the necessary gifts to accomplish this divinely given responsibility, she must keep herself in tune with the Lord's Spirit. She must be spiritually active in the ways the Lord has counseled: regular and rigorous scripture study, focused and meaningful prayer, consistent temple attendance, and so on. She must be holy because she is called to protect that which is holy.

CONCLUSION

President Spencer W. Kimball stated, "There can be no heaven without righteous women."[89] He added: "To be a righteous woman is a glorious thing in any age. To be a righteous woman during the winding up scenes on this earth, before the second coming of our Savior, is an especially noble calling. The righteous woman's strength and influence today can be tenfold what it might be in more tranquil times."[90] We appear to have arrived at the day President Kimball envisioned. Recruits are desperately needed—in the Church, in the family, and in society.

In an era of the world's history in which the family is under attack, the traditional roles of men and women are scoffed at, and the importance of men and women sacrificing for the spiritual well-being of their posterity is derided as antiquated, a frank acknowledgment of Christ's expectations of His followers is desperately needed. The manifest disrespect of both genders in the media and in public discourse is at an all-time high. Men are being reared on a steady diet of sexually provocative images that degrade women and harm how men view and treat the daughters of God.

Much has been said in this small work about how men and women can better follow the counsel of the Lord and His holy prophets and how we can each improve our personal Christianity. Certainly no one should get overwhelmed by what has been presented. King Benjamin wisely counseled, "See that all these things are done in wisdom and order; for it is not requisite that a man should run faster than he has strength" (Mosiah 4:27). The appropriate response to what has been offered herein is *not* to get overwhelmed. Rather, the appropriate response is to pick one or two things the Lord would have you change—things He would have you do just a bit better—and slowly work on implementing the counsel the prophets and apostles have given. While the Lord does not expect total perfection from any of us right now, and the Atonement of Christ is real and present for our shortcomings, we should each, nevertheless, seek the ideal. And the ideal we so desperately need in this fallen world is a return to virtuous women raising children and honorable men who reverence and respect their wives and mothers. The surest ways to stem the tide of disrespect, disregard, and moral decay in our society are to re-enthrone God in the lives of our citizens and re-enthrone women in the hearts and minds of men. A society that truly loves God and sees His face and attributes in His mortal daughters is a society that "shakes at the appearance of sin" (2 Nephi 4:31). It is a society that can "abide the day of His coming" (Malachi 3:2).

We cannot be certain whether Christ actually delivered the aforementioned discourse during the time of His mortal ministry, but we *do* know that the content of it is true and harmonious with things He has said through His prophets over the centuries. As He Himself stated, "whether by mine own voice or by the voice of my servants, it is the same" (D&C 1:38). Now we must heed His counsel.

APPENDIX A

Lost and Additional Scripture in Latter-day Saint Tradition

L atter-day Saints are wont to point out to our friends of other faiths that our use of the Book of Mormon finds justification in the Bible, which time and again mentions inspired works that were once considered authoritative but are now missing from the Christian canon. Examples of books referenced in the Old Testament, but not found therein, include:

The Book of the Covenant (Exodus 24:7).
The Book of the Wars of the Lord (Numbers 21:14).
The Book of Jasher (Joshua 10:13; 2 Samuel 1:18).
The Book of Samuel (1 Samuel 10:25).
The Acts of Solomon (1 Kings 11:41).
The Book of Samuel the Seer (1 Chronicles 29:29).
The Book of Nathan the Prophet (2 Chronicles 9:29).
The Book of Shemaiah the Prophet (2 Chronicles 12:15).
The Acts of Abijah (2 Chronicles 13:22).
The Story of Eddo the Prophet (2 Chronicles 13:22).
The Book of Jehu (2 Chronicles 20:34).
The Sayings of the Seers (2 Chronicles 33:19).
The Book of Enoch (Jude 1:14).
The Book of Remembrance (Malachi 3:16; Cf. Moses 6:5).

Like the Old Testament, the New Testament also makes reference to scriptural texts that apparently were authoritative within the Church during the first century but are not in our Bible today. As examples, the following Pauline epistles are referenced but absent from the New Testament:

- Paul's third Epistle to the Corinthians (1 Corinthians 5:9).
- An additional Pauline Epistle to the Ephesians (Ephesians 3:3).
- Paul's Epistle from Laodicea (Colossians 4:16).

Even the Book of Mormon suggests that scriptural texts have been lost or inspired words have occasionally gone unrecorded or uncanonized. For example:

- The Words of Zenock (1 Nephi 19:10; 3 Nephi 10:16; Helaman 8:20).
- The Words of Neum (1 Nephi 19:10; 3 Nephi 10:16).
- The Words of the Prophet Zenos (Jacob 5:1; 6:1; Alma 33:3; 34:7; Helaman 15:11).

In the Book of Ether we learn that though a complete account of the Jaredites was penned, Moroni did not include "the hundredth part" of that in the Book of Mormon. Thus, for we of the latter days, those details are lost. Of course, the Book of Mormon also suggests that certain parts of the scriptures have been intentionally expunged of divine truths (for example, 1 Nephi 13:26; compare Moses 1:31). In addition to things once accepted but now lost, in Latter-day Saint belief there are also sacred scriptures yet to be discovered—inspired texts that were never part of the canon. Thus, in reference to the Nephites, Jesus told the Jews of the Eastern Hemisphere that He had "other sheep" which He needed to visit and teach (John 10:16). They would record His words to them. To His disciples in the Americas, Christ declared:

> I have other sheep, which are not of this land, neither of the land of Jerusalem, neither in any parts of that land round about whither I have been to minister. For they of whom I speak are they who have not as yet heard my voice; neither have I at any time manifested myself unto them. But I have received a commandment of the Father that I shall go unto them, and that they shall hear my voice, and . . . therefore I go to show myself unto them. (3 Nephi 16:1–3)

Jesus indicated that God had sent Him to speak to many peoples, which Jesus then commanded to make a record of His teachings.

> For I command all men, both in the east and in the west, and in the north, and in the south, and in the islands of the sea, that they shall write the words which I speak unto them; for out of the books which shall be written I will judge the world, every man according to their works, according to that which is written. For behold, I shall speak unto the Jews and they shall write it; and I shall also speak unto the Nephites and they shall write it; and I shall also speak unto the other tribes of the house of Israel, which I have led away, and they shall write it; and *I shall also speak unto all nations of the earth and they shall write it.* (2 Nephi 29:11–12, emphasis added)

Of this passage and its implications for the Church, Joseph Fielding McConkie and Robert L. Millet wrote:

If one people to whom Christ speaks is required to write . . . his words, then it follows as the night follows the day that a like commandment will be given to all to whom he speaks . . .

The Nephites kept their own scriptural record, as have all of the scattered branches of the house of Israel which were led away by the Lord. It appears that [like Lehi and Ishmael] other families . . . were led from time to time by the hand of the Lord to various places throughout the earth. They would have kept scriptural records which will someday be restored to us.[91]

Thus, the Savior's ministry was not limited to the Jews of the Eastern Hemisphere and the Nephites of the Western. As Alma reminded us, "The Lord doth grant unto *all nations*, of their own nation and tongue, to teach his word, yea, in wisdom, all that he seeth fit that they should have; therefore we see that the Lord doth counsel in wisdom, according to that which is just and true" (Alma 29:8, emphasis added).

We do not know the names of all those to whom the Lord revealed Himself nor the extent of the books that He caused them to write. Nevertheless, we do have ample scriptural attestation that these lost and inspired books exist and will, at some future date, be revealed to the Lord's faithful. As Elder Neal A. Maxwell taught:

Many more scriptural writings will yet come to us, including those of Enoch (see D&C 107:57), all of the writings of the Apostle John (see Ether 4:16), the records of the lost tribes of Israel (see 2 Nephi 29:13), and the approximately two-thirds of the Book of Mormon plates that were sealed: "And the day cometh that the words of the book which were sealed shall be read upon the house tops; and they shall be read by the power of Christ; and all things shall be revealed unto the children of men which ever have been among the children of men, and which ever will be even unto the end of the earth" (2 Nephi 27:11). Today we carry convenient quadruple combinations of the scriptures, but one day, *since more scriptures are coming*, we may need to pull little red wagons brimful with books.[92]

While the Apocrypha is not deemed "scripture" by the Latter-day Saints, the Lord reminded the Prophet Joseph that "there are many things contained therein that are true" and "whoso is enlightened by the Spirit shall obtain benefit therefrom" (D&C 91:1, 5). The reason for this positive pronouncement on a book that does not find a place in our officially recognized scriptures is to be found in the words of Moroni: "For behold, the Spirit of Christ is given to every man, that he may know good from evil; wherefore, I show unto you the way to judge; for everything which inviteth to do good, and to persuade to believe in Christ, is sent forth by the power and gift of Christ; wherefore ye may know with a perfect knowledge it is of God" (Moroni 7:16). Thus, those things which inspire us to look to God, to be like God, to treat others like God, are of God, "for good cometh of none save it be of me" (Ether 4:12). Many an inspired text that has the Spirit's seal of approval on its content exists outside of our canon. The ancient text examined herein may be one such document, for its content finds support among the teachings of both ancient and modern prophets.

APPENDIX B
The Legitimacy of Notovitch's Claims

Can we say with certainty that Jesus actually delivered the discourse the monks claim He did? Of course we cannot. However, the question itself misses the point of this book. The content of the words attributed to Jesus in this purportedly ancient text finds support in the words of modern prophets and apostles. Thus, if Jesus didn't deliver this discourse in the first century, He certainly has spoken the ideas contained in it through His living oracles in this dispensation. The words are true, regardless of when Jesus first articulated them.

There has been some controversy as to whether these ancient writings actually exist. Could Notovitch, the man who claimed to have discovered the scroll, have simply made the content of the texts up? Bart Ehrman, an American academic who has become rather famous for his challenges to Christianity, makes the claim that Notovitch faked the entire account, and that *every scholar knows this to be so*.[93] However, Ehrman's recitation of the events leading up to Notovitch's discovery is inaccurate on many points. Several times in his description of the discovery of the document, Ehrman either gets the story wrong or intentionally misrepresents Notovitch's claims.

In addition, he avoids telling his readers about other eyewitnesses whose experience and testimony support Notovitch's claims and contradict Ehrman's position. Since the eyewitness accounts are published, one would assume Ehrman would be familiar with them. However, he only mentions individuals who doubt Notovitch's story. He never speaks of the handful of individuals who themselves made their way to the monastery, saw the texts, and heard the lamas confirm Notovitch's account.

So, for example, Ehrman mentions Max Müller's doubts that Notovitch's story was true, but he does not tell us that one of Müller's close friends, Swami Abhedananda, actually made a trek to the Hemis monastery in 1922 and confirmed the Russian journalist's claims. Abhedananda viewed the text and received a confirmation from the monks that Notovitch had been there and that the document contained what the members of the monastic order believed were original teachings of Jesus. With the help of the lama attending him, Abhedananda translated a portion of the manuscript and published portions of it in his own book.[94]

Ehrman also claims that one scholar "proved" that Notovitch had never been to the monastery. However, the very source Ehrman cites, J. Archibald Douglas, actually said that while the lama denied Notovitch's visit, he had actually been able to prove the Russian journalist had been there by talking to individuals who had interacted with him during his visit—including a medical doctor who had treated the Russian traveler. Thus, Ehrman appears to hold back important details in an attempt to make Notovitch's story appear false.

Related to this last point, Notovitch argued that the Orientals he interacted with often saw Westerners as untrustworthy opportunists, who would, if the chance arose, take advantage of them. Thus, the monks tended to keep "close to the vest" details of things they held sacred or valuable, fearing what Western visitors would do if they learned of the existence of such sacred texts. According to Notovitch, only those who had the confidence of the monks learned of such matters. He noted how hesitant they initially were to share with him. However, after being among them for a time, he was able to gain their confidence and thus access to the manuscripts. Notovitch was not alone in saying that the people of the region were hesitant. Another who saw the ancient manuscripts recorded that "first there was complete denial [regarding their existence]. . . . Then slowly, little by little, . . . creeping fragmentary reticent details, difficult to obtain. Finally it appears . . . the old people in Ladak have heard and know."[95] Another source noted that the monastery at Hemis "seems to attract far more visitors than any monastery in Ladakh. . . . This tends to produce on the part of the monks a superstitious attitude and even outright contempt, and they seem convinced that all foreigners steal if they can."[96] Thus, one's approach would certainly affect how forthcoming the monks were. By Douglas's own account, he took a rather direct and aggressive approach to inquiring about the existence of the manuscripts and the visit of Notovitch. This may have provoked the outright denial by the monk, which Douglas himself acknowledged turned out to be a lie.

Beyond Müller's friend Abhedananda, there were others who made the trek and confirmed Notovitch's account.

Professor Nicholas Roerich made a trek from 1924 to 1928 and encountered oral traditions and written texts that supported Notovitch's claims. Edward Noack, fellow of the Royal Geographic Society of London, visited the Hemis monastery in the 1970s and was told by the monks of the manuscript. Two eyewitnesses spoke of a room at the monastery known as the "Dark Treasury" where a "considerable collection" was "locked away" from public view—and which was usually only opened when one "treasurer" handed over responsibility for the documents to his successor.[97] Elizabeth G. Caspari visited the monastery in 1939, and she was both shown a manuscript and also told of its witness of Jesus. Given the nearly inaccessible location of the monastery, it is quite remarkable how many have made their way there, have learned of the oral tradition regarding Christ and the texts that testify of him, and have had the opportunity to actually see the documents.

Again, this ultimately makes no difference for our study. The content of the discourse is supported by modern prophetic utterance. We cite the purported ancient discourse of Christ here because it provides a good springboard into our discussion of what the Savior has taught through modern prophets and apostles, not because we wish to make any claims about the antiquity or authenticity of the discourse.

ENDNOTES

1 Eliza R. Snow, "O My Father," in *Hymns of The Church of Jesus Christ of Latter-day Saints* (Salt Lake City: Deseret Book, 1985), Hymn #292.

2 C. S. Lewis, *The Weight of Glory*—A sermon preached at the Church of St. Mary the Virgin, Oxford University, June 8, 1942.

3 David O. McKay, *Gospel Ideals* (Salt Lake City: Bookcraft, 1998), 353.

4 Nicolas Notovitch, *The Unknown Life of Jesus Christ,* fourth edition, translated by Alexina Loranger (Chicago: Indo-American Book, 1916), 8.

5 Notovitch (1916), 56.

6 See Notovitch (1916), 9, 94–94, 96.

7 See Notovitch (1916), 152, 153.

8 See Notovitch (1916), 93, 151.

9 "Issa" or "Isha" is the Hindusthani name for Jesus. See Swami Abhedananda, *Journey Into Kashmir and Tibet*, Ansupati Dasgupta and Kunja Bihari Kundu, translators (Calcutta, India: Ramakrishna Vedanta Math, 1987), iv; Per Beskow, *Strange Tales About Jesus* (Philadelphia: Fortress Press, 1983), 58.

10 See Notovitch (1916), 90–91, 93.

11 See Notovitch (1916), 173.

12 For a brief discussion regarding the historicity of the text and Notovitch's discovery of it, see Appendix B.

13 It was not until 1880, during the administration of President John Taylor—and more than 36 years after the death of Joseph Smith—that the Book of Abraham became canonized scripture for the Latter-day Saints.

14 For a discussion of the Latter-day Saint position on lost scripture and inspired texts outside of our scriptural canon, see Appendix A.

15 This version of Christ's discourse is an amalgamation from two different translations. See Notovitch (1916), 136–138; Elizabeth Clair Prophet, *The Lost Years of Jesus: Elizabeth Clair Prophet On the Discoveries of Notovitch, Abhedananda, Roerich, and Caspari* (Malibu, CA: Summit University Press, 1984), 215–16.

16 Again, we speak of the ideal. We acknowledge that there are those who have been abused, neglected, or abandoned by their parents. Those who willfully do such things are not they of whom Christ speaks. His command to respect, reverence and love is to those who have been blessed with parents who have sought to do their best in rearing them in righteousness and treating them with love.

17 James R. Clark, complier, *Messages of the First Presidency of The Church of Jesus Christ of Latter-day Saints*, six volumes (Salt Lake City: Bookcraft, 1965–1975), 6:178, emphasis added.

18 Matthew Cowley, *Matthew Cowley Speaks: Discourses of Elder Matthew Cowley of the Quorum of the Twelve of The Church Of Jesus Christ of Latter-day Saints* (Salt Lake City: Deseret Book, 1954), 76. See also McKay, *Gospel Ideals*, 453–54.

19 McKay, *Gospel Ideals*, 452.

20 See Brigham Young, in *Journal of Discourses* 1:67.

21 Joseph F. Smith, *Gospel Doctrine* (Salt Lake City: Bookcraft, 1998), 313.

22 Clark, *Messages of the First Presidency of The Church of Jesus Christ of Latter-day Saints*, 6:178.

23 Heber C. Kimball, in *Journal of Discourses* 6:125, emphasis added.

24 James E. Faust, "Challenges Facing the Family," in *Worldwide Leadership Training Meeting: The Priesthood and the Auxiliaries of the Relief Society, Young Women, and Primary* (Salt Lake City: The Church of Jesus Christ of Latter-day Saints, 2004), 2.

25 Ezra Taft Benson, *The Teachings of Ezra Taft Benson* (Salt Lake City: Bookcraft, 1998), 543.

26 See Boyd K. Packer, "For Time and All Eternity," *Ensign*, November 1993, 21.

27 McKay, *Gospel Ideals*, 133.

28 Julie B. Beck, "A 'Mother Heart'," *Ensign*, May 2004, 77.

29 M. Russell Ballard, "Daughters of God," *Ensign*, May 2008, 108.

30 Brigham Young, in *Journal of Discourses*, 13:34.

31 J. Reuben Clark Jr., "To Latter-day Saint Mothers," an address given in the Salt Lake 21st Ward, Sunday, May 14, 1933, cited in *Relief Society Magazine*, May 1942, 293.

32 Russell M. Nelson, "Our Sacred Duty to Honor Women," *Ensign*, May 1999, 38.

33 Smith, *Gospel Doctrine*, 314–15.

34 Ballard, *Ensign*, 108–10.

35 Ruth H. Funk, "Come, Listen to a Prophet's Voice," in *Ensign*, November 1978, 107.

36 Smith, *Gospel Doctrine*, 281.

37 Ibid., 288.

38 Joseph B. Wirthlin, "Come What May, and Love It," *Ensign*, November 2008, 28.

39 James E. Faust, "Instruments in the Hands of God," *Ensign*, November 2005, 115.

40 Bruce R. McConkie, *Mormon Doctrine*, second edition (Salt Lake City: Bookcraft, 1979), 118.

41 Nelson, *Ensign*, 38.

42 Ezra Taft Benson, "The Honored Place of Woman," *Ensign*, November 1981, 107.

43 Bruce R. McConkie, "Our Sisters from the Beginning," *Ensign*, January 1979, 63.

44 Harold B. Lee, *The Teachings of Harold B. Lee* (Salt Lake City: Bookcraft, 1998), 250. Elder Ballard similarly taught: "Marrying a good wife is the key to any man's success." M. Russell Ballard, "Elder Ballard is busy, always well-organized," in *Church News,* March 8, 1980, 4.

45 Vaughn J. Featherstone, "A Champion of Youth," *Ensign*, November 1987, 27.

46 Brigham Young, *Journal of Discourses,* 12:194.

47 Thomas S. Monson, *Teachings of Thomas S. Monson*, Lynne F. Cannegieter, compiler (Salt Lake City: Deseret Book, 2011), 331.

48 Cowley, *Matthew Cowley Speaks: Discourses of Elder Matthew Cowley of the Quorum of the Twelve of The Church of Jesus Christ of Latter-day Saints*, 76.

49 Russell M. Nelson, "Women—Of Infinite Worth," *Ensign*, November 1989, 22.

50 Hugh B. Brown, "The Exalted Sphere of Woman," in *Relief Society Magazine*, December, 1965, 888.

51 Boyd K. Packer, *Mine Errand from the Lord: Selections from the Sermons and Writings of Boyd K. Packer* (Salt Lake City: Deseret Book, 2008), 516.

52 Smith, *Gospel Doctrine*, 283–84.

53 Stephen L. Richards, "The Responsibility of Relief Society Members to their Homes and the Priesthood," in *Relief Society Magazine*, December 1951, 799.

54 Lee, *The Teachings of Harold B. Lee,* 251.

55 Ibid., 256.

56 Ibid., 251.

57 Ibid., 252.

58 Ibid., 255.

59 Gordon B. Hinckley, fireside, Copenhagen, Denmark, 14 June 1996, in *Ensign*, August 1997, 4.

60 Gordon B. Hinckley, *Teachings of Gordon B. Hinckley* (Salt Lake City: Deseret Book, 1997), 697.

61 Featherstone, *Ensign*, 27.

62 Richard G. Scott, "Obtaining Help From the Lord," in *Ensign*, November 1991, 85.

63 Laura Schlessinger, *The Proper Care and Feeding of Husbands* (New York: Harper Collins, 2004), xvi.

64 Hinckley, *Teachings of Gordon B. Hinckley*, 690.

65 Gordon B. Hinckley, "Rise to the Stature of the Divine Within You," in *Ensign*, November 1989, 98.

66 *The Family: A Proclamation to the World*, paragraphs 6 & 7.

67 Brigham Young, *Discourses of Brigham Young*, John A. Widtsoe, complier (Salt Lake City: Bookcraft, 1998), 197.

68 Ezra Taft Benson, "Salvation—A Family Affair," in *Ensign*, July 1992, 2.

69 Hinckley, *Teachings of Gordon B. Hinckley*, 695.

70 Lorenzo Snow, *The Teachings of Lorenzo Snow*, Clyde J. Williams, compiler (Salt Lake City: Bookcraft, 1998), 135.

71 Brigham Young, in *Journal of Discourses*, 8:222.

72 Joseph A. Merrill, in Conference Report, April 1946, 29.

73 Karen Jo Torjesen, *When Women Were Priests: Women's Leadership in the Early Church & the Scandal of their Subordination in the Rise of Christianity* (San Francisco: Harper San Francisco, 1993), 259. See also 260–62.

74 Joseph Fielding Smith, *Doctrines of Salvation*, 3 volumes (Salt Lake City: Bookcraft, 1998), 2:70.

75 Leland Ryken, James C. Wilhoit, and Tremper Longman, III, editors, *Dictionary of Biblical Imagery* (Downers Grove, IL: InterVarsity Press, 1998), 247; Richard J. Clifford and Roland E. Murphy, "Genesis," in Raymond E. Brown, Joseph A. Fitzmyer, and Roland E. Murphy, eds. *The New Jerome Biblical Commentary* (New Jersey: Prentice Hall, 1990), 12; J. H. Hertz, *The Pentateuch and Haftorahs*, second edition (London: Soncino Press, 1962), 9. Beverly Campbell defines "help meet" as "a power or strength equal to" man. See Beverly Campbell, *Eve and the Choice Made in Eden* (Salt Lake City: Bookcraft, 2003), 24.

76 Ellis T. Rasmussen, *A Latter-day Saint Commentary on the Old Testament* (Salt Lake City: Deseret Book, 1993), 12. See also

Jacob Neusner, *Genesis Rabbah: The Judaic Commentary to the Book of Genesis* (Atlanta: Scholars Press, 1985), 180; Adam Clarke, *The Holy Bible Containing the Old and New Testaments . . . with a Commentary and Critical Notes*, six volumes (New York: Methodist Book Concern, n.d.), 1:45.

77 Derek Kidner, *Tyndale Old Testament Commentaries: Genesis* (Downers Grove, IL: InterVarsity Press, 1967), 65; E. A. Speiser, *The Anchor Bible: Genesis* (New York: Doubleday, 1962), 17; John H. Sailhamer, "Genesis," in Frank E. Gaebelein, editor, *The Expositor's Bible Commentary.* Twelve volumes (Grand Rapids, MI: Zondervan, 1976–1992), 2:46; Hertz (1962), 9; Vivian McConkie Adams, "Our Glorious Mother Eve," in Joseph Fielding McConkie and Robert L. Millet, editors, *The Man Adam* (Salt Lake City: Bookcraft, 1990), 97. Jolene Edmunds Rockwood translates the Hebrew for help meet as "a power or strength equal to man." See Jolene Edmunds Rockwood, "The Redemption of Eve," in Maureen Ursenbach Beecher and Lavina Fielding Anderson, editors, *Sisters in Spirit* (Chicago: University of Illinois Press, 1992), 16.

78 Rockwood (1992), 16.

79 See Tertullian, "Against Marcion" 2:4, in Thomas Oden, editor, *Ancient Christian Commentary on Scripture—Genesis 1–11* (Downers Grove, IL: InterVarsity Press, 2001), 64.

80 Leslie F. Church, *The NIV Matthew Henry Commentary in One Volume* (Grand Rapids, MI: Zondervan, 1992), 7.

81 George Albert Smith, *The Teachings of George Albert Smith*, Robert and Susan McIntosh, compilers (Salt Lake City: Bookcraft, 1998), 115.

82 Smith, *Gospel Doctrine*, 283.

83 Snow, *The Teachings of Lorenzo Snow*, 135.

84 Richards, *Relief Society Magazine*, 799.

85 *The Family: A Proclamation to the World*, paragraph 7.

86 Smith, *Gospel Doctrine*, 288.

87 Ibid., 313.

88 The same could be said for any woman and how she treats others.

89 Spencer W. Kimball, "We Need a Listening Ear," *Ensign*, November 1979, 6.

90 Spencer W. Kimball, "Privileges and Responsibilities of Sisters," *Ensign*, November 1978, 103.

91 Joseph Fielding McConkie and Robert L. Millet, *Doctrinal Commentary on the Book of Mormon*, four volumes (Salt Lake City: Bookcraft, 1987–1992), 1:352–53.

92 Neal A. Maxwell, *A Wonderful Flood of Light* (Salt Lake City: Bookcraft, 1990), 18, emphasis added.

93 See Bart Ehrman, *Forged: Writing in the Name of God—Why the Bible's Authors Are Not Who We Think They Are* (New York: Harper One, 2011), 280–83.

94 Ashutosh Ghosh, *Swami Abhedananda: The Patriot-Saint* (Calcutta, India: Ramakrishna Vendanta Math, 1967), 41; Abhedanand, *Journey Into Kashmir and Tibet,* 117–19. See also iv–v.

95 Nicholas Roerich, *Altai-Himalaya* (New York: Frederick A. Stokes, 1929), 172.

96 David L. Snellgrove and Taduesz Skorupski, *The Cultural Heritage of Ladaka* (Boulder, Co: Prajña Press, 1977), 127.

97 See Snellgrove and Skorupski, 127.

BIBLIOGRAPHY

Abhedananda, Swami. *Journey Into Kashmir and Tibet*. Ansupati Dasgupta and Kunja Bihari Kundu, translators. Calcutta, India: Ramakrishna Vedanta Math, 1987.

Adams, Vivian McConkie. "Our Glorious Mother Eve." Joseph Fielding McConkie and Robert L. Millet, editors. *The Man Adam*. Salt Lake City: Bookcraft, 1990.

Ballard, M. Russell. "Elder Ballard is busy, always well-organized." *Church News*, March 8, 1980.

_____. "Daughters of God." *Ensign*, May 2008.

Beck, Julie B. "A 'Mother Heart.'" *Ensign*, May 2004.

Beecher, Maureen Ursenbach, and Lavina Fielding Anderson, editors. *Sisters In Spirit*. Chicago: University of Illinois Press, 1992.

Benson, Ezra Taft. "The Honored Place of Woman." *Ensign*, November 1981.

_____. *The Teachings of Ezra Taft Benson*. Salt Lake City: Bookcraft, 1998.

_____. "Salvation—A Family Affair." *Ensign*, July 1992.

Beskow, Per. *Strange Tales About Jesus*. Philadelphia: Fortress Press, 1983.

Brown, Hugh B. "The Exalted Sphere of Woman." *Relief Society Magazine*. December, 1965.

Brown, Raymond E., Joseph A. Fitzmmyer, and Roland E. Murphy, editors. *The New Jerome Biblical Commentary.* New Jersey: Prentice Hall, 1990.

Campbell, Beverly. *Eve and the Choice Made in Eden.* Salt Lake City: Bookcraft, 2003.

Church, Leslie F., editor. *The NIV Matthew Henry Commentary in One Volume.* Grand Rapids, MI: Zondervan, 1992.

Clark, J. Reuben, Jr. "To Latter-day Saint Mothers." An address given in the Salt Lake 21st Ward, Sunday, May 14, 1933. *Relief Society Magazine*, May 1942, 293.

Clark, James R. *Messages of the First Presidency of The Church of Jesus Christ of Latter-day Saints.* Six volumes. Salt Lake City: Bookcraft, 1965–1975.

Clarke, Adam. *The Holy Bible Containing the Old and New Testaments . . . with a Commentary and Critical Notes.* Six volumes. New York: Methodist Book Concern, n.d.

Clifford, Richard J., and Roland E. Murphy. "Genesis." In Raymond E. Brown, Joseph A. Fitzmmyer, and Roland E. Murphy, editors. *The New Jerome Biblical Commentary.* New Jersey: Prentice Hall, 1990.

Cowley, Matthew. *Matthew Cowley Speaks: Discourses Of Elder Matthew Cowley Of The Quorum Of The Twelve Of The Church Of Jesus Christ Of Latter Day Saints.* Salt Lake City: Deseret Book, 1954.

Ehrman, Bart D. *Forged: Writing in the Name of God – Why the Bible's Authors Are Not Who We Think They Are.* New York: Harper Collins, 2011.

Faust, James E. "Challenges Facing the Family." *Worldwide Leadership Training Meeting: The Priesthood and the Auxiliaries of the*

Relief Society, Young Women, and Primary. Salt Lake City: The Church of Jesus Christ of Latter-day Saints, 2004.

_____. "Instruments in the Hands of God." *Ensign*, November 2005.

Featherstone, Vaughn J. "A Champion of Youth." *Ensign*, November 1987.

Funk, Ruth H. "Come, Listen to a Prophet's Voice." *Ensign*, November 1978.

Gaebelein, Frank E., editor. *The Expositor's Bible Commentary.* Twelve volumes. Grand Rapids, MI: Zondervan, 1976–1992.

Ghosh, Ashutosh. *Swami Abhedananda: The Patriot-Saint.* Calcutta, India: Ramakrishna Vendanta Math, 1967.

Hertz, Joseph. *The Pentateuch and Haftorahs.* London: Soncino Press, 1962.

Hinckley, Gordon B. "Rise to the Stature of the Divine Within You." *Ensign*, November 1989.

_____. Fireside, Copenhagen, Denmark, 14 June 1996. *Ensign*, August 1997.

_____. *Teachings of Gordon B. Hinckley.* Salt Lake City: Deseret Book, 1997.

Kidner, Derek. *Tyndale Old Testament Commentaries: Genesis.* Downers Grove, IL: 1967.

Kimball, Heber C. Discourse given December 13, 1857. Salt Lake City, UT. *Journal of Discourses* 6:122–29.

Kimball, Spencer W. "Privileges and Responsibilities of Sisters." *Ensign*, November 1978.

_____. "We Need a Listening Ear." *Ensign*, November 1979.

Lee, Harold B. *The Teachings of Harold B. Lee*. Salt Lake City: Bookcraft, 1998.

Lewis, C. S. *The Weight of Glory*. A sermon preached at the Church of St. Mary the Virgin, Oxford University, June 8, 1942.

Maxwell, Neal A. *A Wonderful Flood of Light*. Salt Lake City: Bookcraft, 1990.

McConkie, Bruce R. *Mormon Doctrine*. Second edition. Salt Lake City: Bookcraft, 1979.

_____. "Our Sisters from the Beginning." *Ensign*, January 1979.

McConkie, Joseph Fielding and Robert L. Millet. *The Man Adam*. Salt Lake City: Bookcraft, 1990.

_____. *Doctrinal Commentary on the Book of Mormon*. Four volumes. Salt Lake City: Bookcraft, 1987–1992.

McKay, David O. *Gospel Ideals*. Salt Lake City: Bookcraft, 1998.

Merrill, Joseph A. Conference Report. April 1946.

Monson, Thomas S. *Teachings of Thomas S. Monson*. Lynne F. Cannegieter, compiler. Salt Lake City: Deseret Book, 2011.

Nelson, Russell M. "Women—Of Infinite Worth." *Ensign*, November 1989.

_____. "Our Sacred Duty to Honor Women." *Ensign*, May 1999.

Neusner, Jacob. *Genesis Rabbah: The Judaic Commentary to the Book of Genesis*. Atlanta: Scholars Press, 1985.

Notovitch, Nicolas. *The Unknown Life of Jesus Christ*. Fourth edition. Alexina Loranger, translator. Chicago: Indo-American Book Company, 1916.

Oden, Thomas, editor. *Ancient Christian Commentary on Scripture—Genesis 1–11*. Downers Grove, IL: InterVarsity Press, 2001.

Packer, Boyd K. "For Time and All Eternity." *Ensign*, November 1993.

_____. *Mine Errand from the Lord: Selections from the Sermons and Writings of Boyd K. Packer*. Clyde J. Williams, compiler. Salt Lake City: Deseret Book, 2008.

Prophet, Elizabeth Clair. *The Lost Years of Jesus: Elizabeth Clair Prophet On the Discoveries of Notovitch, Abhedananda, Roerich, and Caspari*. Malibu, CA: Summit University Press, 1984.

Rasmussen, Ellis T. *A Latter-day Saint Commentary on the Old Testament*. Salt Lake City: Deseret Book, 1993.

Richards, Stephen L. "The Responsibility of Relief Society Members to Their Homes and the Priesthood." *Relief Society Magazine*, December 1951.

Roberts, Alexander, and James Donaldson, editors. *Ante-Nicene Fathers*. Ten Volumes. Peabody, MA: Hendrickson Publishers, 1994.

Rockwood, Jolene Edmunds. "The Redemption of Eve." In Maureen Ursenbach Beecher and Lavina Fielding Anderson, editors. *Sisters In Spirit*. Chicago: University of Illinois Press, 1992.

Roerich, Nicholas. *Altai-Himalaya*. New York: Frederick A. Stokes, Co., 1929.

Ryken, Leland, James C. Wilhoit, and Tremper Longman, III, editors. *Dictionary of Biblical Imagery*. Downers Grove, IL: InterVarsity Press, 1998.

Sailhamer, John H. "Genesis." In Frank E. Gaebelein, editor. *The*

Expositor's Bible Commentary. Twelve volumes. Grand Rapids, MI: Zondervan, 1976–1992. 2:1–284.

Schlessinger, Laura. *The Proper Care and Feeding of Husbands.* New York: Harper Collins, 2004.

Scott, Richard G. "Obtaining Help From the Lord." *Ensign,* November 1991.

Smith, George Albert. *The Teachings of George Albert Smith.* Robert and Susan McIntosh, compilers. Salt Lake City: Bookcraft, 1998.

Smith, Joseph F. *Gospel Doctrine.* Salt Lake City: Bookcraft, 1998.

Smith, Joseph Fielding, Jr. *Doctrines of Salvation.* Three Volumes. Salt Lake City: Bookcraft, 1998.

Snellgrove, David L. and Taduesz Skorupski. *The Cultural Heritage of Ladaka.* Boulder, Co: Prajña Press, 1977.

Snow, Eliza R. "O My Father." *Hymns of The Church of Jesus Christ of Latter-day Saints.* Salt Lake City: Deseret Book, 1985. Hymn #292.

Snow, Lorenzo. *The Teachings of Lorenzo Snow.* Clyde J. Williams, compiler. Salt Lake City: Bookcraft, 1998.

Speiser, E. A. *The Anchor Bible: Genesis.* New York: Doubleday, 1962.

Tertullian. "Against Marcion." Alexander Roberts and James Donaldson, editors. *Ante-Nicene Fathers.* Ten Volumes. Peabody, MA: Hendrickson Publishers, 1994. 3:269–474.

The Family: A Proclamation to the World. The Church of Jesus Christ of Latter-day Saints, 1995.

Torjesen, Karen Jo. *When Women Were Priests: Women's Leadership in the Early Church & the Scandal of their Subordination in the Rise of Christianity.* San Francisco: Harper San Francisco, 1993.

Wirthlin, Joseph B. "Come What May, and Love It." *Ensign,* November 2008.

Young, Brigham. Discourse given April 8, 1852. Salt Lake City, UT. *Journal of Discourses* 1:66–71.

_____, Discourse given October 21, 1860. Salt Lake City, UT. *Journal of Discourses* 8:222–226.

_____, Discourse given June 18, 1865. Salt Lake City, UT. *Journal of Discourses* 11:119–128.

_____, Discourse given April 6, 1868. Salt Lake City, UT. *Journal of Discourses* 12:192–196.

_____, Discourse given April 8, 1869. Salt Lake City, UT. *Journal of Discourses* 13:29–37.

_____, *Discourses of Brigham Young.* John A. Widtsoe, complier. Salt Lake City: Bookcraft, 1998.

SCRIPTURE INDEX

Doctrine and Covenants

Pearl of Great Price

TOPICAL INDEX

ABOUT THE AUTHOR

Alonzo L. Gaskill is a professor of Church history and doctrine at Brigham Young University. He holds a bachelors
degree in philosophy, a master's in theology, and a PhD in
biblical studies. Brother Gaskill has taught at BYU since 2003.
Prior to coming to BYU, he served in a variety of assignments
within the Church Educational System—most recently as the
director of the LDS Institute of Religion at Stanford University (1995–2003).